THROUGH THE LOOKING GLASS

A LOVE STORY

Bobbi O'Connor

THROUGH THE LOOKING GLASS

A LOVE STORY

Bobbi O'Connor

DEDICATION

To my father, Mike O'Connor
To my beautiful, crazy, loving mother, Teresa Mary
McGregor Davies O'Connor
To Malcolm Edward MacDonald, surrogate father,
mentor and friend

LOVE IS A ROSE

Love is a red rose
A beautiful flower
Surrounded by thorns
Yours only to see and feel
Not to grasp tightly to your breast
Lest thorns pierce
Blood flows from heart to ground
Your love lost....

~~Bobbi O'Connor 2017

INTRODUCTION

THIS IS A STORY OF HOPE. A true story of a young woman coming of age as she deals with mental illness and eventually attains both emotional and mental health. I hope the story will engage and encourage other young women and men as they grapple with mental health issues. These issues are becoming more and more prevalent among youth in our stressful and crazy society.

Join me as I go through trials and tribulations, and learn many lessons in life, over and above all the "book learning" I received in my career.

The moral of my story is that if you are true to yourself you can find love in this world.

Names have been changed to protect the privacy of all the players in my life – both the "good" guys and gals and the "bad" guys and gals. Although in my opinion, there are no good guys (gals) or bad guys (gals), just human beings, who are fallible and make mistakes.

This book was originally written as an intimate letter to a person who journeyed with me. The intent was to fill in the gaps for him so he could see these past events from my perspective and thereby let him into my soul.

I apologize if at times the narrative is hard to understand, cryptic or disjointed. I have tried to provide explanation so my story can be shared with you, the reader, as well.

Enjoy your reading.

~~Roberta (Bobbi) O'Connor

FOREWORD

THE AUTHOR OF THIS STORY did some work projects for me and I subsequently did a couple for her. Our relationship was at times somewhat tumultuous but always respectful.

This narrative is quite flattering to me. To explain: whenever I have a working relationship with a woman, she is **always** "out of bounds" for me. These relationships are always "professional". Respect and admiration must be the primary emotional factors for me within a working relationship. I too, learned a lot in this process.

The part of Bobbi's story I appreciate most is her description of her relationship with her husband, Karl – and the elements which make it work so well. for them.

In addition, I know this couple makes a significant contribution to our society and I pray that they will continue to do so.

~~ Malcolm Edward MacDonald

Table of Contents

THE MEETING

I REMEMBER THE DAY WE FIRST MET. It was in December 1978. I documented it, in my diary, as I documented all my meetings and contacts while researching Gary Freeman's Fraser River fishing bar inventory. You were working at the Fish and Wildlife Branch, as a recreational planner. I remember you sitting at your desk, a compact man, with a good head of black hair and brown eyes.

When you noticed I was paying more attention to you than to what you were actually telling me about what the job entailed; and what I had come to learn; you gave me a look with those brown eyes. You let me know that you knew I was not paying attention.

THE SUMMER

SLIPPING INTO INSANITY

I REMEMBER WHEN GARY'S PROJECT was over in April. Even the volunteer part was completed by the end of March, I was sitting in my farmhouse home in Port Coquitlam, slipping into depression, because I didn't have a job anymore.

The phone rang. You were on the other end. You offered me a job with the Fish and Wildlife Branch. I gladly accepted and started in May 1979.

I went to your office and met you again. I was very interested because I remembered my original attraction to you. But this time when I met you, I noticed right away you had a ring on the third finger of your left hand. You were married. Rats!

I don't know where I learned specifically; or what influenced me; perhaps my parents' fidelity to each other; or the teachings of the catechism by the nuns and others; but there was a clear boundary in my mind that one (meaning me) did not get involved with married men. So I didn't.

So on to work. You explained the job description. It was a detailed account of topographical mapping to which I had never had any experience or introduction.

I was very stressed and nervous listening to you, and couldn't remember what you had said. I asked you to repeat it – which you did. I began to notice stress through that experience. This is when I felt my personality first split.

I went to work on the project you gave me… however, now there were two of us in my head. One was a somewhat angry person while the other was a beautiful, loving young woman.

The two persons were like my father (the angry one) and my mother (the loving one). I thought after all those years of hearing them fight constantly, I had become like them, in my mind.

I had always been very shy and was scared to talk to people. This resulted in my being very lonely at times. However now I had someone; an intimate friend; with whom to discuss all sorts of things. I walked around the office … not talking to anyone… or even meeting their eyes… because I didn't want them to see what was going on in my head. But in my mind I was carrying on conversations with this other person. I finally had a friend.

The beautiful young woman refused to harbour romantic thoughts about you – even though she was in love with you – because that would have been impure thoughts – which her religious teaching said was wrong. However she fantasized that had she had a son; he would have looked just like you; and she poured all her love towards you in that capacity.

How could she know you would have looked like the son she never had? Her first lover was dark… darker than you… a man from a far away country… from a city called Nairobi. He was about your height and build.

The relationship did not end well, and she took a pill to wash away the seed. Or perhaps she was never pregnant. But in her heart wished she had been. The guilt and remorse followed in the back of her mind… hidden from thought even… for years.

The other angry person was not so enamoured of you. "She" didn't like you at all.

The loving person said, "He's a nice man."

But "she" (the angry one) wasn't convinced. However, there was never any conflict where one of us wanted to do one thing and the other another thing. We just talked and carried on a mental conversation between "she" and I.

THE BREAK

IT WAS THE LAST DAY OF MY STINT at the Fish and Wildlife Branch. You had asked to meet with me, so I could show you all the material I had compiled for you. I was very proud, and very happy to get this time with you. Over the summer, you were gone most of the time, and usually too busy to spend more than five minutes talking to me about work.

We met in the lunch room and I was showing you all the stuff I had worked on and completed. I went through it in detail with you when a young man (I say young, because I am much older now, but, he was about my age, then in his twenties) came in. I had seen him talking to you previously at the Serpentine Fen.

You said to him, "I thought I told you to meet with me on Wednesday."

It was a Tuesday that day. And for me – Black Tuesday. He replied he couldn't make it on Wednesday. I can't remember exactly how he worded it. You went back and talked with him while I sat there. I heard you talking with him about a job he was to start with you very soon.

It is hard to explain now… but I can still remember those desperate times… with no family or backup. I was at the end of a job and hoping to get even a short term contract… if one was available.

I figured, "You are trying to get rid of me, and told this guy to come in the day after I was finished so I wouldn't know about it."

But now I had found out. I felt deceived, betrayed, and angry.

I thought, "That guy does not even respect you and yet you give him a job over me."

The young man left, and we resumed going over the work I had done for you. But now there was two of us in my head.

The angry one was thinking, "I'm going to punch that guy (meaning you) in the head."

But "she" knew you were a good fighter, and "she" would only get one chance.

So while we were talking, "she" imagined winding up and punching you in the side of your head… just for practise.

But just before the imagined fist hit your head, an imaginary hand came in between, and the nice one said, "Don't do that, you'll hurt him."

The angry one was frustrated and couldn't do anything. As I finished off talking to you, the words were like sawdust in my mouth. You praised me and said how well I had done … but I did not believe you. You had lost credibility with me… not for giving someone else a job… which was your right … but for the deception.

As I turned and left, I thought to myself,

"At least there is a guy in Chilliwack, who likes me."

As I will explain in the next chapter, I was grasping for any guy, because I was so desperately lonely.

BUDDING ROMANCE ?

I FIRST MET HIM AT DOUGLAS LAKE, during the softball tournament for Fish and Wildlife Branches, I attended with Marilyn, a co-worker, and several others. It was a brief encounter… a bit strange… but, I thought he had a sense of humour.

(I couldn't have been more wrong).

After returning to the office, and while I was working, he phoned me and said:

"This is… (and gave me the name of a famous biologist)."

I am afraid I didn't get the significance of this statement. The name of the famous biologist was unfamiliar to me as I was new to the Fish and Wildlife Branch.

But he only phoned me once. I was hoping he would ask me out, but I didn't hear from him again. All I really knew about him was that he worked for the Fish and Wildlife Branch in Chilliwack.

The summer waned on, and in August, word was in the office that someone called Damian Gudnicht had planned a barbeque at his home in Chilliwack and invited everyone from the office.

I was not much interested, as I was not a party person, (being very shy) and did not mix well. However when I was minding my own business working away at my desk, Terence Weatherby, one of the biologists, came over to me and said there was a phone call for me – at his phone.

I went to the phone and it was Damian Gudnicht inviting me to his barbeque. Notes were distributed in the office with directions to his place. Chilliwack seemed a long way off to me and I didn't know the way.

On at least one or two more occasions, Terence Weatherby again came to my desk with a phone call from Damian Gudnicht, inviting me to his barbeque. I wasn't really interested, however but I started to get the impression they really wanted me to come to their barbeque. I thought maybe the guy I was interested in… whom I knew was from Chilliwack… perhaps had put them up to it… but was maybe too shy to ask me himself. As I said, I was lonely and grasping at straws for a relationship.

It was probably common knowledge in the office – but I was not aware that he also lived with Damian Gudnicht – or I would have been forewarned and more cautious – and perhaps seen or felt a set up.

THE BARBEQUE

THE DAY OF THE BARBEQUE, I got up early and went to the Pheasant Farm out in Pitt Meadows. I was helping Gary Freeman and his crew set up nets for the pheasants. We worked all day in the hot sun without any food as I recall.

While I was there, in the afternoon, Marilyn came by with her escort George Fidstrom, and asked if I was going to Damian Gudnicht's barbeque. I had planned to at this stage, but in retrospect, it seems a bit strange that she made a trip out to see me at the Pheasant Farm to push the invitation. Not knowing her involvement… it is all speculation in any case.

I went home to get ready, but did not have anything to eat before I left, as I assumed there would be food at the barbeque. I arrived out in Chilliwack early, before very many people had arrived.

A volleyball net was set up in the yard. I had a cup of white wine, on an empty stomach, and it probably went straight into my bloodstream. I didn't feel it however. I just felt a bit relaxed. A few people arrived, then my "love interest" arrived and came up to me. He took my hand and led me around the side of the house.

I figured he just wanted to kiss me or something like that. We got around to the back of the house, and he put his hand against my chest and pushed me down on my back, and fell on top of me. He started groping me immediately.

My heart fell. I had hopes of his being a boyfriend…but even in my limited experience… I saw this for what it was. I sank into a depression, (I think because of the wine as well) and stayed frozen.

In my previous experience … when my psychopathic brother did stuff like this to me… I had always found it was better to lay still… or he would get violent and perhaps beat me up. I lay still, frozen because this seemed to be the only protection I had ever had, like a bird caught by the stare of a large feline.

So it went on for a while. I wanted to get away, but didn't know who to yell for help to. I could hear Terence Weatherby talking (he had a very loud voice) and thought maybe I would yell for help.

Then I remembered, "He helped set this up, he won't help you."

Then I thought of you. I remembered how that guy had come in and taken the job I wanted, and you had deceived me.

I thought, "I don't think he really cares, one way or the other."

So I didn't call to you for help.

The groping went on and on, and I just wanted to get away. Finally, I started to lift my shoulders from the ground to get up (even with his weight on me) and that is when it happened.

He switched ends on me and put his mouth on my private parts. The stimulation was overwhelming. Suddenly I lost control and couldn't stop doing it. I had a hallucination. Because of the strong feelings I saw blood pouring from my arms. All the guilt that was pent up in me over the years just flowed out.

I looked up and saw your young son watching, and tried to grab him. He was too fast and ran away. But, because I knew he saw it… afterwards… I was sure you knew what had happened. I believed your small son would have told you.

When this sexual assault stopped, I lay there just wanting to get away. But he wouldn't get off me.

He kept saying… "I live here." Stay with me tonight." (or something to that effect), over and over and over again.

I heard everyone leaving the party and thought "I will never see any of these people again, I want to say goodbye to them."

So I said to him I would 'sleep' with him… although I just said it to get rid of him… and when I said it he immediately jumped up and ran away.

I went to find you immediately, to complain about my treatment by this guy to you. You were talking to

17

Marilyn who sat on a table with her legs spread provocatively. I waited behind you but I didn't know if you noticed me or not. I thought you knew I was there and were just ignoring me.

I waited and waited and waited, and then suddenly I looked at myself and thought "He won't talk to you because your clothes and hair are all messed up".

So I went to my car, where I had a change of clothes and put on my jeans and a shirt, and combed my hair. I went to the kitchen to look for food, but everything was gone. I had not eaten since early morning.

By that time, you were crouching down in the grass, playing with your little boy. I waited for you to speak to me. I was unable to speak first to you. I just wanted to say goodbye at this point, and tell you how much I had enjoyed working with you.

You didn't look up but gave me a friendly wave of the hand. Part of me knew this was a friendly wave but the other person in my head didn't take it that way.

"She" was angry and whirled away, with "her" back to you.

"She" told me, "I told you he was like that" and was very angry with you

The nice one said, reluctantly, "I guess you're right."

"She" decided to 'sleep' with that guy after all… to spite you… and embarrass you in front of your friends.." (As if that hadn't happened already that night, ha, ha).

The nice one thought, "Then I could get pregnant and have a baby and I would have something to take

18

care of that no one could take away from me… as you had taken the job away from me… despite the fact I had worked all summer and did a good job."

I also had the thought that if I could prove to you I was promiscuous… you would spend hours talking to me… as you had spent with Marilyn… as I believed you knew she was promiscuous also. But, that was only a sarcastic thought to myself.

I didn't really expect to have anything to do with you after that night. In short, I had lots of reasons to do what I did. But I knew it was the wrong thing to do. However, I had split and let "her" take over. To stop "her" at that point would have resulted in a violent explosion.

I noticed you waited for me to come with you, but the window of opportunity for you to speak to me had passed so I refused your help.

THE LONG NIGHT

TOWARDS THE END OF THE LONG NIGHT
(morning), my personality switched back to the nice
one. To his credit… he asked… and I did not respond
verbally.

I thought to myself "I don't want to have sex with
you and I certainly don't want to have your child."

(I guess I was like Bill Clinton. I didn't consider
that what had transpired as being sex).

Mercifully that was enough and no pregnancy
resulted.

AFTER THE BALL

FOLLOWING THE BARBEQUE, the balance of power had changed in my mind. The angry one was now dominant and in control. The nice one could only follow along. She was scared of what the angry one had planned.

The angry one had been frustrated, but planned to go to the downtown eastside and search out men for sex. Very scary indeed.

The nice one wanted to phone you for help, and the angry one allowed the call, because "she" didn't think you could do anything to stop "her" at this point. "She" was in control.

I phoned you and all I could think of was to ask you for a reference, as I thought at least you could recognize and acknowledge I had done a good job. The angry one was like a little nymph or goblin over my shoulder as we talked, gloating. I heard the shock in your voice.

In the meantime, I got a job at the fish laboratory in North Vancouver, and moved my residence to Coquitlam, to be closer to work. Luckily, and I will repeat *luckily*, I also paid the post office to have my mail forwarded to my new address.

I was working for a few weeks… I can't recall how long… when I came home and got your reference letter in the mail. I opened it eagerly (not for the job reference)… as I knew it was a message from you… my last chance. And you didn't let me down.

I could read that you were upset with me, "Please feel free…" however that had no effect, as I had heard so much abuse during my young life from my father, that I was hardened.

It was the last sentence that held me, "If you need any advice, etc. etc. please consider me as a resource person."

In that instant, the nice person took control over the angry person again.

Strongly. I felt that I was a young thoroughbred filly. A filly who had taken the bit in her mouth and was running away out of control. You were behind me with a can of oats and corn,…rustling it,… and calling me back.

And as I heard the oats, I slowed down, and thought, "Well, I am quite hungry", and came back to you.

But I didn't contact you back and I continued to work at the fish lab. A few days later… as I was cutting up fish heads… the angry one was brooding as we worked. "She" complained about how you had stopped "her" from heading downtown to get sex from lots of men. "She" was very angry with you as "she" thought about it.

Someone said something to "her", which set "her" off, and "she" started yelling and waving the knife. "She" was yelling at you... but you weren't there so "she" didn't do anything. But if you were there, "she" would have gone after you with the knife.

The nice one kept control to the point where she wouldn't allow the angry one to search out men and sex since the nice one had found love. However the angry one was powerful enough to take us away... and ran away to visit some friends in Alberta, who had moved there recently.

The nice one kept control, but still had to go along. Also my mother was noticing something was going on and asking questions. I didn't want her to know the state of my mind, so I had to leave.

ALBERTA BOUND

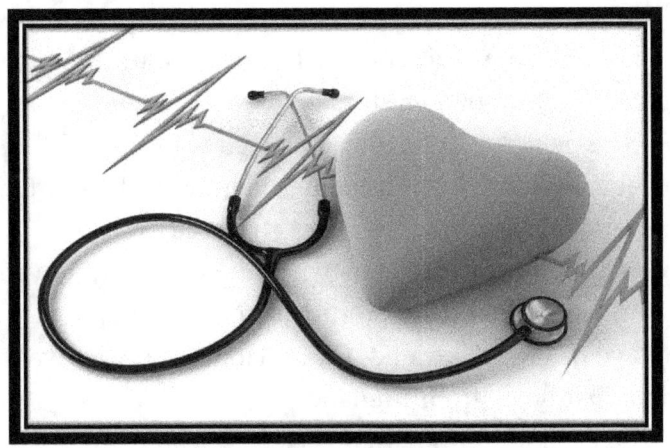

A TIME OF HEALING

I RECEIVED A SPEEDING TICKET just outside of Kamloops and pulled over a bit later into a small motel, and negotiated a night's stay with the proprietor for $18 – a discounted rate. He could see if he didn't lower the rate I would drive on. As it was off season, he agreed to it.

In the morning, I headed for Alberta from B.C. I phoned my friends from Revelstoke, and met my friend Diana Clarkson, at the Red Rooster store in Rocky Mountain House. She led me to their farm, 15 miles out in the countryside.

I was able to hide my personality split. Diana didn't suspect anything and just treated me as the young friend she had always known. I was able to maintain a "front" (which was my nicer self).

They fed me wonderful chicken dinners almost every night. I gave their two young daughters riding lessons and helped out on the farm with their goats. They lived in a house trailer on the acreage which they had bought from their cousin. There was a little cabin in the back – without a washroom – where I slept.

The next day or so after I arrived we went horseback riding. I had trained a chunky Arab-Quarter horse cross mare, who was very stubborn, in basic training with some dressage while the Clarkson's lived in Port Coquitlam. I was fortunate to have had the tutelage of Diana's friend, Claire Horsmann who was a riding instructor from England.

Over time I progressed very well with my own riding coupled with the training of the mare Shoo-Shoo – or as she was called in the show ring, Shosha Vuba. She was responsive and a pleasure to ride. We rode along the gravel roads through the countryside for several miles basking in the warm glow of the autumn sun. Near the end of the ride we stopped in at a new friend of Diana's. (Diana was a very social person) She had prepared a wonderful spread for us. We dined and then resumed our ride home. It was a wonderful experience. I still remember this day very clearly.

I was only there for about two weeks when the Clarkson's had a family emergency. Sam, Diana's husband, had kidney failure and we had to rush him to Edmonton to the hospital. Diana and I and the children went back to the farm. Diana visited him a few times a week.

Their truck broke down so she used my car to go back and forth. I looked after the children and the farm while she was away. Sam came back after a few weeks outfitted with a type of dialysis or treatment. It was a bag on his stomach which drained, or medication was inserted into. I'm not sure now but this contraption was prone to allowing infection into his body. He had to be very careful.

One day in early October I woke up and it was snowing. Such a surprise as this never happened so quickly at this time of year in Vancouver. I was now trapped in Alberta. My old, green, little compact Datsun was not serviceable enough to drive back in the snow.

In fact, Diana's cousin, who had been a helicopter mechanic in the Vietnam war, said he could hear from the sound of the engine that I should never have left Vancouver in it for such a long trip. After Sam came back home, the Datsun finally broke down and I had to get it fixed. Unfortunately the Clarkson's did not offer to pay towards this expense although they had been using it regularly.

I had to get a job in order to stay in Alberta for the winter. I found a job in a nearby pottery shop for $4/hour and worked there for a few weeks. In the meantime I was staying with the Clarkson's. They served wonderful meals and I wolfed them all down.

In fact in retrospect, I think I was eating in one meal what normally would have lasted them for a few days for the whole family.

Sam approached me one day, and said, "You're eating too much of our food, and you'll have to pay rent to us." (Not an unreasonable statement in the circumstances).

However it was his disrespectful tone and the fact he did not acknowledge I had let him use my car along with working on the farm and taking care of everything while he and Diana were in hospital in Edmonton.

The experience I had in Chilliwack came back and I thought, "I'm not going to put up with more abuse from Sam. He's a acting like a jerk. "

So I went into Rocky Mountain House and looked for another job.

I went from business to business, and talked to the proprietors. Finally I got a job at an oil field supply store which was run by a man named Randy. He said he hired me because I had told him I had a farm background in Vancouver and he knew farm girls worked hard.

I commuted the 15 mile drive to and from the Clarkson's every day. But it didn't seem far. It was all through the farmlands with no traffic. Randy's store was very successful at the time (1979) and had grossed over 1 million dollars worth of business in the previous year as Randy confided in me.

Randy had a wife and a couple of children They owned a quarter section of land which had been given to them by Randy's in-laws. However, it was not enough to support his family, So he "worked away"… running the oilfield supply store.

He had another worker, I can't remember his name. He was a silent Ukrainian fellow who did all the parts work. I did the reception desk and the bookkeeping which I think I learned on the job. I had never done that kind of work before.

We went on until Christmas, when I got my picture and name in the local paper, as Randy was interviewed for his store and we all posed for it. I still have that clipping.

I can't remember the exact month, but in that time frame there was a provincial election. Randy knew I was NDP and it was a big joke in the office. He talked politics with me and laughed about it.

When I asked for time off to go and vote he allowed me to leave in the middle of the day because he said "The NDP are not going to win anyways – so go ahead!"

(Now in 2016 the tables are turned, the NDP is in power in Alberta, and the oilfield supply stores are probably out of business or not doing so well – especially after Fort McMurray's disastrous fire.)

I went home to Port Coquitlam for Christmas with the plane ticket my mother sent me. I bought a lot of stuff from the pottery shop where I had worked as gifts for my brothers and sister and parents.

The plane from Calgary went straight up over the mountains and then straight down into Cranbrook. It was a bit hairy or should I say scary. I was lucky my bag of heavy pots did not bring the plane down. Perhaps that is why the plane had such trouble getting over the mountains.

When I went back I did not stay at Clarkson's. I stayed at a motel for a few days. I got a call from the mother of a family friend of Clarkson's, Elizabeth, who asked me to look after her dogs while she went to Mexico for a holiday. I could stay in her house while she was gone. I gladly accepted.

It was about 10 miles outside of Rocky Mountain House and on the other side of town. I had to carry my car battery into the house every night just to keep it warm as there was no plug in. Sometimes I dripped acid on my jeans. When I went back to Vancouver, folks might have noticed most of the jeans I wore had holes in them. (I understand that is the fashion now! Ha, ha).

One day my car would not start, so I walked two miles down the drive to the road in -20 Fahrenheit weather. I noticed by the time I got to the road, my knees were congealing and walking became difficult.

Luckily I was able to flag down a ride to Rocky Mountain House and arrived at work. I was that determined to work… no matter what. No one was there. I was very cold from the long walk. I was on time, so I climbed in the shop through a small window (I was very slim, then). Randy was a bit surprised when he got there, and probably a bit concerned over me doing that.

After Elizabeth got back from Mexico (she had vacationed with Sam's father, David Clarkson, who was a widower, I needed a place to live again.

One of the customers, Bob Short, whose family had lived in Rocky Mountain House since the beginning of the town practically, asked me to take care of his elderly mother, and to live with her. I also gladly accepted this offer. It was closer to work as she lived in town. I had brought my dog from B.C. and he had to stay in the basement, as she would not allow a dog in the house. Consequently I was not happy there.

Her son Fred Short, would often drop by in the evenings to talk to his mother and I gather he was attracted to me. He offered to marry me and said we could go to Fort St. John and farm in the Peace River country. I declined as gracefully as I could because I already had you in my heart. There was no room for anyone else. It was an interesting offer however. What do you think?

I had an opportunity to rent a house of my own. I found, through the oil field supply store contacts that there was a house for rent down the street from the store, for about $300 or $400 per month. (I can't remember exactly how much it was).

I went to the owner who ran a Greek restaurant in town and rented the house. It was a two storey house, with bedrooms on the upper floor and a kitchen and living room on the lower floor There were railway tracks running nearby. I can't remember if it was an active track. I don't think it was as I don't remember any train sounds. In the evenings there were a lot of Native Indians hanging around the bush area of the tracks.

I needed a place to keep my dog during the day once I moved to the town of Rocky Mountain House while I was at work. I heard there was a kennel just outside of town. I found it and went there and made arrangements to board my dog there for $15/day. He was a black and white Springer spaniel/lab cross. He was very high strung with a lot of mental issues and an annoying incessant bark.

Sue and Harold ran the local kennel which was also the town pound. They were a blended family, as Sue had previously been married to a tall, big man who was physically abusive. She had a tall, large daughter of about 10 years of age, who was also very aggressive.

Harold had been married to a Native girl, and had two children, both boys. Sue had raised the younger boy from an infant when she had got together with Harold. Together they had a fourth child, a little girl of about 2 years old.

When I moved into the house, I found that sometimes I got a knock on the door from the homeless Native Indians or other people living in the bush around the tracks. My dog was useless as he was so nervous he would hide under the bed, when they came. So I went to Sue and Harold one day, and asked them if they had any dogs I could adopt.

I knew they had a full house of impounded dogs, and was hoping to adopt a nice Husky.

The day I talked to Sue, she said, "We just killed all our dogs today. We couldn't keep them any longer as the Town of Rocky only pays for a certain time," (It may have been a few weeks).

They had kept them long after that time, but couldn't afford to carry them any longer. Sue said, however, we do have one dog left, and she is very well trained. She is a blue-tick hound cross. She was left behind when someone moved, and howled for days in the cold before we picked her up.

When we took her into the vets to be euthanized, she dropped like a rock on the outside door mat and wouldn't move. We couldn't get her into the vets. We stepped over her, carrying the other dogs to be killed.

At the end, we were so tired of killing, that we said, "Let's spare her, perhaps we can find her a home".

So I met Daisy. She wasn't called Daisy then, that is what I called her afterwards. My mother had a habit of making up songs for each of her children, so I remembered the song,

> **"Daisy, Daisy, give me your answer true.**
> **I'm half crazy over the love of you. It**
> **won't be a stylish marriage. I can't afford**
> **a carriage. But you'll look sweet, upon the**
> **seat, of a bicycle built for two."**

She was an affectionate, you might call "sucky" dog, and somewhat selfish. She had a very thin coat and to keep warm at night she slept on the sofa with me, often stretching her legs out in the middle of the night and pushing me off the sofa. She also had a very loud bay, which she would let loose if she heard a noise, and scared away any potential intruders.

One day my landlord appeared at my door. He said he wanted to move into the house with me as he had had a fight with his girlfriend. I was shocked. I didn't respond to him right away because I sure didn't want this. He shoved past me and came into the house. He went upstairs.

I will laughingly tell you what he found there. (I never went upstairs, I lived in the bottom floor only). I had let Daisy out every morning to do her business but had not accompanied her. Unbeknownst to me, she would not do her business outside, as it was too cold for her. Instead she went upstairs and did her business there.

So when the landlord went upstairs, there were several piles of dog doo in the bedrooms.

He stormed downstairs, and said angrily to me as he left, "Get rid of that dog!"

So Daisy saved me again. I didn't get rid of her. I never heard from him again about moving in. Whew!

In the meantime, in the new year, things were going wrong at the oil field supply store. I was doing a good job as far as I know – but I was not happy. I didn't want to be doing "office work" which I looked down on as "woman's work".

I wanted to be doing the parts work, which I saw as "man's work". However the Ukrainian had the job nailed down and they didn't consider me for this although I think I may have made some attempts to help out.

I started to become paranoid. I could feel it coming and I think I was rude to some customers. I knew I wasn't doing well.

Randy came to me one day and said "I'll have to fire you".

I understood, because I knew I had some problems. I didn't hold it against him. But it was a shock nevertheless.

I left the shop that afternoon and went to the kennel to pick up my dog. I was crying because I had lost my job.

When I stepped into Sue and Harold's trailer home, they said "Why are you crying?" I replied "I have lost my job at the oil field supply store."

They responded with, "We need a helper at the pound, a dog catcher and kennel maid, can you do this for us? We will pay you $8/hour."

My spirits were lifted immediately, and I stopped crying. I gladly accepted their offer. This experience taught me to be resourceful and self reliant. I learned not to be defeated by the ups and downs of life – in particular of employment.

As my motto is now, "One door closes and another door opens."

So the next day I started cleaning kennels and dog catching. It was not easy cleaning kennels, as they were frozen and I literally had to chip out the ice bit by bit. But I did it and did a good job. Sue and Harold were happy with me and I became friends with them.

Dog catching was another story. I don't think I excelled in it. I remember one day I was out in a neighbourhood and a pack of huskies ran by. There was no way I could catch them. Even if I did, I didn't know if I could handle them.

However, there was a little Chihuahua in the road outside a house which I picked up. I went to the house and knocked on the door to return the dog to the owner. No one answered.

I took the dog back to the kennel and Sue said "If no one picks the dog up in a few weeks, we will adopt it out."

Sue said likely no one would pick it up as people in town did not want to pay the pound fee. I think it eventually was adopted out, but I thought it was sad that someone lost their little pet. However if I had left it in the road, it might have frozen to death.

The night after I was fired from the oil field supply store, I remember I was still very sad. I was in the upper part of town around six or seven o'clock at night. It was dark and -20 Fahrenheit, but I was warm, because I was wearing the wool coat my mother had knitted for me the previous year.

I was leaning against a power pole, and thinking of another 'firing' where I had lost my job with you. Emotion welled up in me and I wept for how I had treated you. All the abuse I had experienced over the years of growing up welled up inside me and came out. I finally cried and cried.

I had become hardened it seemed. This had happened one night when I was a teenager and I had a fight with my father. He said awful things to me that made me cry.

A thought came to me, at that time, "He said that to make you cry and he is taking pleasure in that."

So all the years and all the abuse that followed, I never cried again until that night I cried for you.

I never thought to contact you personally. I was too shy and awkward. I thought about you often.

As the winter ended, I thought of going back home since work at the kennel was petering out. There were not many prospects otherwise in Rocky Mountain House or Alberta for me.

I thought, "You could try phoning Malcolm MacDonald. Maybe he would give you a summer job."

So I phoned you. I think you were happy or relieved to hear from me. In any case you were kind enough to offer this prodigal daughter a job with the British Columbia Fisheries. I thank you for that.

Before I head back to Vancouver in my little green Datsun, I will relate one more story that taught me a life lesson from Rocky Mountain House, Alberta.

One winter day, when there was still snow on the ground, Daisy woke up on the living room sofa. She pushed the front door open. It was not latched very well. She ran up the road and disappeared. I went out to look for her everywhere and couldn't find her.

I phoned Sue at the kennel and told her Daisy was lost.

She said, "Harold has gone to investigate a call for bears at the dump and is with Trapper Jim."

As it turned out the "bears" were Newfoundland dogs. Harold and Trapper Jim took care of them and took them to the kennel. Harold, Trapper Jim, and I ended up at the local bar near to where I lived.

Trapper Jim had many stories and entertained us all afternoon. (Unbeknownst to me, Harold was a wandering husband, but it was well known in the community, apparently)

We drank several jugs of beer that afternoon and had a good time. At the end, I went home, somewhat drunk, and with a staggering gait, and entered my front door.

Daisy was laying on the sofa, nice and warm. The door had been opened and she had found her way back in! I was overjoyed, and I can't remember what I did afterwards, but likely joined her on the sofa for a snooze.

The next Monday (I was still working at the oil field supply store at that time) I talked to a customer, Bob Short, and related my weekend experience.

He said to me "It's lucky you went home, or you wouldn't have found your dog." (Very profound statement).

I gathered from this I had been observed by the townsfolk that afternoon, who knew the potential dangers of my drunken situation although I was still somewhat unaware.

As I said, I got a good education in Rocky Mountain House. It was a time of healing for me.

RETURN TO BRITISH COLUMBIA

RAISED IN THE FISH AND WILDLIFE BRANCH

THE JOB IN BRITISH COLUMBIA was with the
Fisheries Branch. George Strong was the manager. He
was a large stout man, somewhat reminiscent of Burl
Ives, and referred to me as "O'Connor". As in (to my
supervisor) "How did O'Connor do?" He was strict and
knew what he was doing.

The work entailed aquatic resource inventory. I
guess I had had some experience at the time, but never
thought of it that way. This was a bit different from the
fishing bar inventory. It involved the measurement of
physical and biological parameters of streams and lakes.
It was very hands on work.

My first assignment was in Port McNeil, Vancouver
Island. I took the bus to meet my co-worker who was

already up there working. He was dismayed when he met me at the bus stop.

"They sent me a girl!" he wailed. However I was not daunted as he seemed like a fairly nice guy. He was a big moose of a man, smart enough to get along, but not brilliant.

I proved to be of some use. At one lake, there was a hill with bush above the lake and we had trouble getting down to the lake. The "moose" pushed through the bushes and plowed down to the lake but with difficulty.

I tried to push through the bushes but bounced off. I kept moving along the road while pushing into the bushes periodically, until finally the bushes gave way. I had found a trail. Things were much easier after that, carrying the boat and all our equipment down to the lake.

I learned another lesson, that summer too, "Always have a backup."

"Moose" and I were out on the lake all day until evening doing our stream and lake measurements. The last thing we did was to drop a 'maximum-minimum thermometer' to the bottom to the lake to measure the temperature. We raised it gradually and took the temperature at different levels.

As we drew it up, the knot on the string it was tied to slipped, and we could hear the chain, which weighted it, clank all the way to the bottom of the lake.

"Moose" cried out, "Oh, No!"

Sure enough. Our thermometer was at the bottom of the lake.

He said, "George Strong always says to make sure you have a backup."

I responded with, "Do you have a backup?"

He said "Yes, but the other thermometer is in the truck, back on the road."

So we took the boat across the lake, climbed up the trail through the bush to the truck, got the thermometer, traveled all the way back to the boat with the thermometer. We went back on the lake and measured the temperature.

By this time, it was late evening. We did not get back to Port McNeil that night until 11 p.m. and by then all the restaurants were closed and we went hungry.

Lesson Learned: Always have a Backup and Bring it With You! Bring a lunch, too!

I realized then that when I went to Chilliwack that night the previous year, I had had no back up plan, and consequently crashed.

I never made that mistake again, and in my future after Port McNeil, I always have a backup in place for any eventuality.

I didn't have a Visa at the time and had not thought of accommodations. I had left it up to my partner to arrange. When we first went to a motel, my partner, "Moose", realized I had no money or Visa to rent a motel room so he suggested we share the room he had rented.

There were separate beds and he did not bother me. There was no hanky panky going on, you can be assured. In fact he became somewhat irritated that I used up all the towels…Oh well.

George Strong, the boss, did not miss this awkward arrangement. However, the next assignment he sent me on was with a female partner.

Another lesson learned: The staff of the Fish and Wildlife Branch cared for me and were looking out for me.

When I first came back to Vancouver, to see you at the Fish and Wildlife Branch on Manor Street in Burnaby, I knew I had to face the music. I wanted you to know I was really sorry, for any embarrassment I had caused you by my behaviour at the barbeque the previous fall. I dressed accordingly.

In my religious training over the years, in the Bible, it was told that people who were repentant wore sackcloth and ashes. So I found an old rough cotton shirt (of an attractive light green shade) and wore it with some jeans, which had holes in them from the battery acid dropping on them the previous winter in Alberta.

I don't know if you saw the significance of my appearance, but you were kind enough to forgive me, although I could see you were a little mad when I first came in. (You did forgive me, didn't you???) And we moved forward into a new relationship.

You told me things I hadn't thought of before, like the fact that when you have sex with someone, you could pick up all sorts of diseases from them. That helped cool any ardour I may have been experiencing, and made me think "Yuck, I don't want that!"

You teased me about my sexuality, testing me with funny little comments, to see if I was sleeping around or not. And you spent some time talking with me. (I knew

45

if I proved I was promiscuous you would pay attention to me, and it worked).

I held you to ransom somewhat in that regards, as you were not quite sure of what I might do, and wanted to prevent it. In actuality I was quite solidly yours and wasn't looking for anyone else – but I didn't want to let you know that, lest you stop talking with me.

As the next year or so went by, I noticed you were talking to whom I will now call "the formerly angry one", who was like a three year old child. You talked to "her' as you would to a child, and I (the adult one) and "she" (the child) knew you were talking to "her".

I (the adult one) loved you – but "she" (the child) did not. "She" was mistrustful of you and you worked to get "her" trust and confidence. I did not think it was wise for you to develop a relationship with "her"… as I knew what "she" was capable of… but you were determined to.

It was difficult for "her", and "she" tested you often, to see if you were trustworthy. Eventually after about two years, "she" had come to the place where "she" had developed a bond with you, although "she" still had some insecurity.

It was an insecurity somewhat like that of a foster child who has been abused and shuffled from home to home far too many times in a short life time.

But "she" started to thrive in the knowledge that you considered "her" your child. And there was the knowledge and feeling also that the need was mutual, you needed and wanted a female child or daughter as much as "she" needed a father.

FAMILY CONCERNS

ONE EVENING, WHEN WE MET at a pub near your office, you delivered devastating news. In the shadowy room, you told me your wife was expecting a baby. You told me when she found she was pregnant… she was determined to have an abortion if it was a boy… as she wanted a girl only. In that instant, I had a feeling of pure hatred toward your wife, stronger than anything I had ever felt until then and even until now.

I felt that she had gotten pregnant to have a daughter… in order to replace me in your life… to push me out of your life. It had never bothered me that you already had one child because he was a son. I did not consider him competition for your affections, as I was a girl, and it was different.

You told me your wife had undergone amniocentesis and the child was a girl, so she was carrying through with the pregnancy.

The nice part of me (the adult) "thought" to the other, "When the child is born, they will invite you to see her, and it will be like you are part of the family."

But I wasn't sure if that would be the case or whether you were meeting me that night to tell me goodbye.

The child was due in January 1983. I waited for the call… the invitation to come and see the new baby. But it never came. I was intensely curious to see the new baby.

In the spring or early summer, I think it was, I was in Langley on a goat trip of some sort and my truck ran out of gas.

I could have gone to my cousin's who lived nearby you, but I thought I would use it for an excuse to see your new baby. I knocked on your door and your wife answered. I asked her if I could borrow $5 for gas.

She turned to get the money. (I think she was a bit scared of me because I looked rough and was smelly or maybe she was just cautious), but she kept the baby in her arms and went into the house. I was wishing she had left the baby on the floor, so I could pick her up and hold her.

I took the $5 from your wife, thanked her and left.

DEVILS AND DEMONS

COMING TO THE LORD

IN 1983, I WAS WINDING DOWN a Salmonid Enhancement Project. I was managing a project for the Federal Fisheries Department. One of my workers (someone I was supervising and who supervised the crews) was a man called Bill McNab, who had been to the BCIT Fish and Wildlife Program, and was very capable.

I got to know him, and he told me of his upbringing, that his mother had beaten and abused him terribly as a child. Towards the end of the project, I could see he wanted to be romantically involved with me. I confided in a friend of mine… a wife and mother a few years older than me… who was very wise in the ways of families.

She told me if he was abused badly by his mother as he said, he would likely also beat me up if we were married. I took it to heart and didn't get involved with him. However we did have some association and talked at times.

On one occasion, one night when I was taking care of my goats and sheep at my farm in Port Coquitlam, I had hallucinations. Devils and demons were clawing at my feet and trying to trip me up with their long green and purple claws. Bill was with me at the time and I told him what I experienced.

He had been involved with a Christian group in Mission called the Burden Bearers,. He said come with me and I will get help for you. It was a dark and stormy night, and he drove out to Abbotsford. I followed him in my own car.

We knocked on a door, and walked into the home of a young pastoral student at the Theological College in Abbotsford. He was an African by the name of Nnamdi Obasi (we called him Nnam), and his wife, Ngozika Obasi. He had a couple of young children at the time, but they were in bed when we came so we didn't meet them.

Nnam had been a pastor in Africa, traveling from village to village, casting out devils from people in the congregations, and preaching to the people there. He had come to Canada with his wife to get a formal theological education, as a Christian pastor, and was attending the college in Abbotsford at the time.

Nnam talked with me, and I told him what I had seen.

He said, "You are full of devils, and only one thing can be in you at one time, either devils or God."

He asked me if I accepted Jesus Christ as my personal Saviour. I didn't love Jesus Christ, however I had now experienced the devils and demons, and was very scared of them.

So in order to get rid of them, I said, "Yes, I accept Jesus Christ as my personal Saviour."

And at that moment, I felt the devils and demons leaving me, and felt empty and relieved of them.

I started going to church. I was living in a little hollow, on a farm in Aldergrove, near a small one room church. I went there one Sunday and listened to the sermon. The preacher was talking about John the Baptist, and the baptizing of Jesus. He kept repeating some words over and over again. Suddenly – inside that little church – I saw a blue cloudy sky overhead, and heard a big booming voice say:

"This is my beloved son, in whom I am well pleased"

…**and it wasn't the preacher talking!**

THE PASSOVER

"...AND WHEN HE SEETH THE BLOOD ("of the Lamb" - my words) upon the lintel and on the two side posts, the Lord will pass over the door and will not suffer the destroyer to come in unto your houses to smite you." The Holy Bible, King James Version, Exodus 12:23.

It was November 1983. The municipal elections were on, and you told me you were running for alderman in Langley. I always wanted an excuse to be near you, so I asked if you wanted any help. You said I could come and help paint signs and put them up.

I was farming goats and sheep and horses at the time and had a truck. I was always rather smelly, as I was on the farm with the goats, handling and milking them etc. most of the time. However I came and helped you and your wife prepare for the election.

I painted signs in your basement, with your wife, and got to know her a little better. Mostly she talked, I didn't say much, so I don't think she got to know me much at all.

But some of the things she said were interesting, as when she said: "He (Malcolm) is the most honest man I've ever met."

It was clear to me she thought a lot of you.

I offered to help wash the pile of dirty dishes in the sink, but you replied, "Evelyn likes it done a certain way, and likes to do it herself."

I wasn't sure if that was true, or if you thought I was dirty and smelly and didn't want me to handle the dishes. But either way it didn't bother me.

The last night before the election, when I was at your home helping, you and your wife had to go to your relatives in Maple Ridge, to pick up something. I can't remember exactly what it was now. I just remember that you both were going, and asked me if I would baby sit your infant daughter for a few hours.

I heard a small voice in my head say "I didn't really come here to baby sit." It was a very slight, subtle thought, and I didn't think much of it.

I had baby sat many children in my life. It was just part of what I had done as a daughter in my own large family and for other families as well to make extra money. You showed me where the diapers and the bottle and milk were, and you and Evelyn left.

I went to bed, and suddenly when I was laying there "she" (the angry one) came back. "She" started to rant about how you didn't love "her" anymore. I had a brief vision of the baby laying in blood. I took charge and cut "her" off immediately.

I refused to listen to "her", because I knew if I did, "she" would take over my mind and harm your baby. Because "our" minds were so intimately linked ... even though I refused to listen to "her"... I knew what "she" wanted to say... and that is that I had been replaced by your daughter.

I didn't know if this was true or not, I only knew one thing for sure. I loved you with a love deep and pure ...more than anything else in this world... even more than I loved myself... and didn't want to do anything to harm you.

I wanted to go to sleep because I was tired. I knew that I "sleep walked" at times ... and that it was "her" who was present and had more control when I "sleep walked". I had to keep awake and keep conscious control of my mind in order to protect your baby.

I lay there eyes wide open and awake. Then the baby cried. As a baby sitter I could not ignore this cry. I went to the baby, who had a wet diaper and tried to change her in the bathroom. But I couldn't find the right sized diaper, because she was very small and all the diapers I found were big. So I wrapped a large diaper on her.

Next I warmed up the milk on the stove... and fed her and put her back in your bedroom. I was nervous I might harm her the whole time... but managed to keep control. Back in bed, I lay awake waiting for you and your wife to come home.

It took a long time, and when I finally heard you drive up, I was very relieved. Your wife, with a mother's concern, went to her baby immediately to make sure she was alright. You talked to me and I then went to sleep.

Believe me, if I had known I ("she") thought like that, I would never have come to your house to help you and expose your family to such danger. I had no inkling beforehand of how "she" (the angry one) felt.

THE FIGHT

BEING AROUND YOU AT ELECTION time, stirred up memories of what had happened in Chilliwack, and I knew it had been sexual assault–not sexual relations. I had been set up, and wanted to complain to the manager at the Fish and Wildlife Branch, Joe Simpson about his men.

I thought about going there, but didn't know how to explain to him why I had willingly had sex with the guy. I didn't know how to explain to him that I had a "split" personality. I hoped if you went along you could explain that to him.

So I phoned you at your home, as you weren't at work. Your wife answered, and I asked if I could speak to you.

She said "No!" in a snotty sort of way, like *'No, you can't speak to my husband'*.

She didn't say, "He is sick or he has injured himself and is in bed and isn't taking calls, can you call him at the office in a few weeks". She just said, "No!"

So my first desire was to get your wife out of my way so I could talk to you. I told her, "In that case, I'll phone Joe Simpson," knowing full well that she would take that as a threat, which she did.

She started screaming and went to get you. When you answered the phone you yelled at me, "Don't ever phone here again!!!!!!" very angrily and loudly, a response very out of character for you and certainly not expected by me.

When you yelled at me, all the anger in "the angry one" welled up also.

"She" was very angry with you because of your daughter, and thought, "He said not to phone him, but didn't say I couldn't come to his house" (We were always splitting hairs like that with my father, who had very poor discipline over all his children).

The nice (adult) one could have stopped "her", but at that moment thought that perhaps it would be better if you knew how angry "the child" was with you, so that you could protect yourself from "her".

I felt that I was at the verge of losing my control over "her", and needed your help in keeping control. So I let "her" drive over to your house and confront you.

You came to the door and stood outside on the porch. You knew it was "her" right away, and didn't engage in small talk.

You told "her" very firmly, "I want you to go a long way away– and not come back here anymore."

"She" was perplexed as to how you knew it was "her", but had to obey you as you had given a direct command. "She" left in a storm, never to return, and I followed after "her".

I was relieved you had taken care of the situation, and now knew you and your family were safe from "her".

I noticed you were kind enough to say, I could phone you at the office, which was a very generous gesture and not deserved – but I gratefully accepted it.

"She" was still angry with you. It took a month or so to get over it… but "she" did, and I resumed phoning you at the office.

I heard you had injured your shoulder and were in a lot of pain and this is why you had yelled at me.

But I knew deep down inside, you also yelled because I disrespected your wife.

Another lesson learned: "Respect women, Especially your friend's wife."

Behaviour learned over 18 years in an environment where women were disrespected and abused was reversed in one lesson, for life.

An important lesson to learn… as I was a woman myself… and needed to learn to respect women and myself as a woman.

DENOUEMENT

I MOVED FORWARD IN MY INTERNAL life, developing from a 3 year old child to a teenager, although actually I was going on 31 years old. I worked in the bush at Minnekhada Park, building trails with an EI crew, and carrying on as a teenager, flirting from time to time, exploring my limits, and so forth.

Trail building left a lot of time for thought. I mused over what had almost happened and wanted to confess to you. (Part of my Catholic upbringing, I think). It was very difficult however. I finally asked you to meet with me. We went to the Jolly Roger Pub in Pitt Meadows, on your way home to Mission.

My hands were dirty and I first washed them. I ordered a coke.

I started to tell you, and my preamble was "Did you ever realize I had a split personality."

Before I could say more, you said, "I have known that for a long time. What you have is schizophrenia. If you go to a mental health centre, they will give you medication which will cure you."

I was overjoyed to hear this, as I thought a split personality was incurable and I was stuck with it for life. We ended the conversation and you hurried home to your family.

I went to the local mental health centre in Port Coquitlam at lunch time one day. I spoke with the psychiatric social worker, Gloria Neuenhoffer, an older lady who was working at that time.

She asked "Do you ever smoke marijuana?" and I replied "Only occasionally with the crew."

I told her I had schizophrenia and would like some medication for it.

She responded "I will make an appointment with a psychiatrist and a psychologist to test you to see if you have schizophrenia."

I did not let myself get too anxious. I knew that if they wouldn't give me medication, I could get you to phone them. You would tell them yes, I really did have schizophrenia.

You were my trump card and my security. The psychiatrist interviewed me... but as I was on my best behaviour... he could not see anything wrong with me.

Later I went for a written psychological test, which asked all sorts of apparently irrelevant questions, but which indicated clearly I was schizophrenic. I started on medication the following week, and have never looked back nor failed to take my medication.

STARTING A NEW LIFE

A MONTH OR SO LATER, I attended a group therapy session at the mental health centre, recommended by my psychiatric social worker, Gloria Neuenhoffer. I went into the room and sat down. I saw a tall, dark and handsome young man come in. He was very bright, friendly and bubbly in his speech.

I knew when I met him he was the man I wanted to marry. He was wearing a blue BCIT jacket, so I broke the ice by telling him I had attended BCIT also. I hoped he would ask me out for coffee.

We attended two more sessions together over the following weeks, but he didn't ask me out for coffee. So during the third session – thinking that if he quit coming to these sessions, I might never see him again – I took the bull by the horns and asked him for coffee. He accepted, and we went forward in our life together after that.

Because of the life lessons I had learned, we had a long courtship before we became intimately involved.

This is not to mean we didn't share many sweet kisses in the meantime. Later he told me I had forced him to get to know me by making him wait, otherwise I would have been just another conquest, and he would have moved on.

During our courtship we tested each other in different ways, each of us wanting to be sure that the other was The One.

The young man wanted to be intimate from the start, but tried allaying my fears by stating "I would just like a little affection (meaning sex)".

I set the standard by not giving in. By this action I took the chance that he would leave me for a more willing partner. But he didn't leave me. My actions showed him that I thought more of him and myself than just a casual sexual encounter.

We enjoyed many weekend outings together. We went to Ambleside Beach in North Vancouver and other parks by bus. (We were on a budget and didn't have a vehicle). We also visited Expo 86 in Vancouver, Fantasy Gardens in Richmond (Bill Vander Zalm's enterprise), and many other places over the eight years we dated.

While dating and wanting to settle down with someone, I thought to myself "I have spent half my life (I was 35 years old) in abusive situations and I do not want to spend the last half of my life being abused."

I looked for a partner who would treat me kindly and with respect. I looked for a man who treated the most vulnerable, the handicapped, or mentally ill, with kindness and respect also. The young man demonstrated much kindness to those people we met through the New

View Clubhouse, for psychosocial rehabilitation, located in Port Coquitlam. Many of those people as well as the staff at the New View Society became good long term friends of ours.

I chose this man for my life partner despite other more "macho" men trying to get my attention. He is a quiet, unassuming and good man – proud in his own way – and above all a kind person. I accepted only respectful treatment from him and he responded positively and did not leave.

I married him and stuck by him when others counseled me to leave him just because he couldn't get or hold down a job. I married a man – not a job or a position of power.

Our happiest years were when we were most poor. We have each other and love and support each other in every way.

Eventually he brought me home to meet his parents. I was serious about him, and wanted to know the family I was considering being a part of for the rest of my life. I took the opportunity to observe carefully. My own experience and the words of wisdom from my older woman friend, Rose, gave me the knowledge that more than likely how his father treated his mother would be how he treated me once we were together for life.

His father, Frans, was a quiet but ascerbic man. He did not verbally abuse his wife as my own father had done. Marieke, his wife, would make delicious meals for all four of us. His father would tuck into the dinner, thoroughly enjoying it. When he finished he would sit back, take time to pause, and then say to his wife,

"Lekker" which in Dutch means "Delicious." A fine reward for his hard working wife.

I was also aware that the relationship between a young man and his mother would be reflected in how the young man would treat his life partner. His mother was strict, but loving, and the young man respected her in word and actions. In fact, as an only son, he was very devoted to his mother and always put her first.

Another older woman friend told me "He is a mama's boy."

My response was "He treats his mother like a queen and that is how he will treat me once we are married." That has truly been the case.

The ways I feel valued, respected and loved are as follows:

1. He always uses terms of endearment in normal conversation, calling me dear or sweetheart.

2. He always opens the car door for me.

3. He insists on a hug every night when I come home from work.

4. He makes dinner for me every week night.

5. He always takes the garbage out.

6. He does the laundry and feeds the cat in the afternoon.

7. He makes the bed for us every night.

8. He kindly admonishes me when I am upset about something and start swearing ("No sailor language, dear...")

9. When my temper explodes he expresses concern "Are you feeling alright?" and calms me down by his kindness.

10. He does not return an aggressive act in kind but waits until I have calmed down and then says "Would you like a hug?"

11. He lets me make decisions even if they're wrong, and quietly keeps his counsel; waiting until I see the error for myself; then supports me in my change of course.

12. I have been well treated, even spoiled by my husband in our marriage. I have grown emotionally and always tried to reciprocate his love.

My married life is very happy – in stark contrast to my earlier years. We share our bed, our home, our cars, our money, our cat, our lives and our love!

Once you have happiness, all the rest – economic success, financial security, and social position will come in due time – if they are ever to come. And if they don't come you don't care because you already have it ***all.***

So I have a lot to thank you for Malcolm, for bringing me up so well in such difficult circumstances.

I owe you the happiness I presently enjoy with a good and faithful husband, for starters.

I also owe you thanks for teaching me proper behaviour. This has enabled me to have long lasting and gratifying personal and professional relationships in my life.

As I grow older, I find that the most valuable treasures in my life are the relationships I have with others, yourself, and your lovely wife included.

THANK YOU!

POSTSCRIPT

ON WEDNESDAY MARCH 30, 2016 after these memoirs, "Through the Looking Glass," were completed...just a day following a trip to Mission, B.C. to deliver a copy to my friend, Malcolm MacDonald... an amazing coincidence happened.

While I was dropping off a friend near my home... and as we were talking... she brought my attention to two... then three balloons drifting ever higher into the atmosphere... far above the tallest evergreen trees.

My friend said, "There are hearts on those balloons," which appeared red and pink in colour and, visible even from a distance.

I replied, "Those are my Valentine balloons!"

I had given my husband, Karl a bouquet of balloons for Valentine's Day. We had kept them on the dining room table since February 14th. The day before, at the end of March, I had finally disposed of them in the garbage bin.

Someone had likely come a few moments later and lifted the lid and broken the strings tying them down. The helium in the balloons lifted them into the air high above the streets, houses and apartments in White Rock, and South Surrey.

I responded, "This is an amazing coincidence."

It was deeply symbolic and tied into the theme of my recently completed memoirs in a surreal way.

My life has traveled full circle.

My life is a story of love, rejection, and being thrown away… which now rose to these new heights.

It is a story of redemption.

It may not be of interest to any but the Christian believer… but these memoirs were written over the Easter weekend of 2016: from Good Friday to Easter Sunday.

In a further development, while having dinner with a friend of mine on March 31, 2016 (the week after Easter), the waitress informed us her name was 'Epiphany'.

An Easter Miracle… a re-birth!

A New Beginning…

A HAPPY ENDING

Thank you, my friend…
Thank you, Malcolm and your lovely wife…
Thank you, my dear husband, Karl…
Thank you to everyone who helped me along my
journey to health and love…

Dear Reader:

Thank you for your time spent reading this book about my life.

If you enjoyed this book and could relate in any way, please do leave me a review on Amazon or contact me.

I can be reached at:
info@through-the-looking-glass.net

***

NOTES:

NOTES:

NOTES:

NOTES:

_____

_____

_____

_____

_____

_____

_____

_____

_____

_____

_____

_____

_____

_____

_____

_____

_____

_____

_____

_____

_____

_____